Power Texting Men!

The BEST Texting Attraction Book to Get the Guy

Gregg Michaelsen

Power Texting Men!
The Best Texting Attraction Book to Get the Guy

By Gregg Michaelsen
"Confidence Builder"

Copyright © 2014 Gregg Michaelsen

ISBN-13: 978-0615958521
ISBN-10: 0615958524

CONTENTS

INTRODUCING

YOUR CRASH COURSE GUIDE TO TEXTING MEN

Welcome, ladies, to *Power Texting Men!* My name is Gregg Michaelsen, and I feel like this texting guide was a long time coming. Most of us have been texting for at least a decade, but today it's become more important than ever to be **good** at it! You need to know what you're doing, or it's going to be the weak link in your dating life.

The POWER behind this book is that it's written by yours truly... a Guy! And not just any guy, I'm the guy that trains the other side and knows exactly what YOU do wrong. I'm also the guy who knows what turns US on. 1000's visit my website: KeysToSeductions.com every-day so I can help you reel in any man on any subject!

> Gregg's best-selling books work! I've read them all: <u>Who Holds the Cards Now</u>, <u>The Social Tigress</u>, and <u>Love is in the Mouse</u> work seamlessly to give women an arsenal of power to gain the upper hand with MEN!
>
> Allyssa, Boston, MA

Today's special? TEXTING MEN!

Now, plenty of you are genuine textperts at this point. You've been diligently typing away to boys since before you knew what it was you were supposed to do with them. You'd think after so many years of texting you'd have amassed tons of experience, yet you're constantly being surprised by how a single text can spin out of control, become misunderstood, and lead to a relationship flat lining when you know it could have been something more.

You're left wondering what you did wrong, what subtle cue you missed, and what, if anything, you can do to fix it. Take for example this little gem of a text conversation, and take a stab at what you think went wrong in it:

You: Hey qt how r u?

Him: I'm good, and you?

You: Good. What r u doing?

Him: (No response)

You: Want to see a movie 2nite?

Him: Sure. How about Batman?

You: I was thinking more like a porno LOL no jk batman is cool!

Him: (No response)

You: Hello? U ignoring me?

This text conversation is going to need a defibrillator and a team of trauma experts to come back from. And even then it has a snowball's chance in hell without a miracle. I can count at least eight things wrong with it, and since this is so obviously terrible, I'm sure you can see a few mistakes as well; however, I'm going to hold off mentioning what these are. At the end of this book, you're going to come back to this very text conversation and know exactly what mistakes I'm talking about.

The Secret to Great Texting

Did you think I was going to keep you waiting the entire book to give you the ultimate secret to great texting? Hell no, I'll give it to you right here in the prologue! Here it is, plain and simple:

At the core of every amazing relationship (and every great text!) is a conversation built out of challenging the other person.

That demands a bit of an explanation. As human beings we crave growth, and we seek out friends and partners that promote such growth. For that to happen, we must know how to properly challenge our mates. We must also be able to do so in a balanced way, or else you get a whole nasty string of side effects, such as contempt and misunderstanding, that eventually leads to relationship death.

Not good! We've all been there before, and only practice is going to stop it from happening again.

What you need to know right now is that every response is a test, a challenge, because it's this challenge that's going to create an engaging relationship. With the help of this book, you're going to have a plan of attack, a method of staying one step ahead of him. That's an important thing to remember: y**ou always need to be a step ahead!** And I'm going to show you how.

So we have our Golden Rule above, and we know that **challenging** our other half is essential. But why exactly is it important to challenge them? What are the benefits of doing so? To understand that, let's bring out two important side rules, which happen to be the subjects of the first two chapters of the book. When you challenge your partner, two amazing things happen:

A. **You create <u>tension</u>, which is what makes someone interesting. Tension creates <u>attraction</u>,** and

B. **You create <u>respect</u>, which is how you develop importance in someone's eyes. Respect creates <u>value</u>.**

All you need to know at this point is that tension is just another name for flirting, and respect, well, you already know how important that is to maintaining a relationship. But in chapter two, I'm going to show you just how you can create boundaries through texting, which in turn will lead your partner to respect you more.

By the end of the first two chapters, you'll not only understand how to write an amazing text, but you'll know what creates amazing relationships that last forever. I teach you how to challenge your partner in fun ways, to keep a text fun and not boring, to eliminate all things mundane and above all to be flirty and exciting!

Chapters three and four are wakeup calls for any of you ladies that have expressed anything even remotely looking like "need" in a text. Neediness is the death of relationships, both for men and for women. I teach you how to steer clear of it, as well as a number of other major no-no's and common blunders that you should never do under any circumstances.

I bring it all together in chapter five. By then, you'll be an expert regarding the psychology behind the text, and all you'll need are a few hard and fast rules to become the Queen Bee of texting.

A savvy gal understands a few things about how relationships work if she is going to be a master texter. That's why the core of this book focuses on the psychology of male and female relationships, and how we apply them to texting. Just because you can reel out 100 words per minute on your iPhone 5 using your pinkie fingers doesn't mean you've mastered the art of the text. The psychology behind it is going to be what takes you from novice to expert.

Before I close this up, I want you ladies to remember a few important things about texting:

a. It's not going away. We've all been at a point that we

wish that texting would just disappear. Either we sent something stupid or we are impatiently waiting for a text from that person we like. Instead of getting angry, embrace the game! Over the course of the book I'll explain some methods of coming back from bad texts, but the reality is you may be better off learning from your mistakes and moving on.

b. If you're not big on writing, don't worry! You have more time than you imagine you do when you get a text from someone you like. Stop, put the phone down, and give it some thought. You've got all the time in the world!

c. Plenty of you gals imagine that men just throw texts at you and leave it at that. Trust me, they are just as nervous about screwing up as you are. Oftentimes their texts may be more bluntly put than yours, but they do care how you perceive them. You're both nervous!

We're going to address that nervousness of yours starting right now, in chapter one. By the time we're through, you're going to be texting up a storm. You'll be more confident, more capable, and a downright awesome texter!

First off, you and I are going to take a little trip to the wild side of the man's brain. I have a rockin' bunch of seductive teaser texts that every babe needs in her arsenal. GUYS react to these kinds of texts!

Let's get started...

SEDUCTIVE
QUICK START GUIDE
TO TEXTING

My 21 Man Seducing Texts

Hi Girls (Guys take a hike). Here I want to give you my quick guide to tease the crap out of a man by seducing him with only your thumbs... for now!

This chapter is the BOMB to get the guy through texting. Which is why I wanted it right here, front and center, **before** we delve into the core of the book.

This is done by short, seductive messages during the day. These texting gems will trigger emotion in him and get him thinking about you in wild ways. This is the beauty of the male mind, it doesn't take much to get us obsessed about a woman if she teases us properly.

Flirt texting makes us fantasize about you all while your clothes stay on! No Sexting Needed!

Couple of crucial things to remember:

1) *These are powerful, aggressive texts used by women who have abundance in their lives (of men), not scarcity.*

2) *The goal is to stir emotion! This will work on the great majority of men. For the guys that don't get it...well, forget em!*

3) *Texting and ALL things dating only work when a woman is backed by her own self-confidence. Need some? Read my Best Seller: The Social Tigress*

4) *These are single sentence SHORT texts that stand ALONE. They come out of nowhere and they are followed by SILENCE even if and when he responds.*

5) *Follow up hours or days later with my "normal" (but powerful) texting found after this chapter. This process drives him crazy. It makes you mysterious as he can't figure you out and he NEEDS to. The CHALLENGE is born!*

6) *These are based on the assumption that you had a good 1st experience together. Didn't have to be great, just good.*

Here are my examples of flirtatious text messaging that will SNARE him like raw tuna fish to a feral cat:

1. The "I know you want me" text. Send this after your first date or right after you give a guy your number.

> *You: "Play your cards right and things could get interesting"*

You: "I know you miss me, I'll call you soon"

You: "How's it been without me lover boy"

You: "Can't get over me can you?"

You: "You know, there are other girls out there for you"

You: "Who's hotter than me?"

You: "I've got options, what you got?"

You: "So tell me why I should date you?"

You: "The jury is still out on you"

This displays crazy-ass confidence on your part. You are telling this man that he wants you and that you know it. This is highly effective even if he is undecided about you. This is innate to man. You have created a challenge to him out of thin air and he will take the bait.

2. The "Compliment" text.

You: "Your blue eyes were driving me wild last night"

You: "Something about you I find very seductive"

You: "I loved how you handled that situation-made me wet"

You: "That was hot last night when you held my hand"

You: "Don't ever show me that tattoo again or things will get crazy!"

You: "My friends can't stop talking about you"

These are massive compliments to him. They are stated the PROPER way. He will get excited just wondering what the future holds with you. Any of these texts fills his mind with questions, all of which, he can't answer:

- Does she say this to every guy or does she just like me?

- What is she like in bed?

- Is she really that observing?
(I better do things right the next date)

Be careful with these as they don't contain any slight insults (negs, I call them.) You don't want him thinking he has you at his beck and call. So be sure to swing the "pendulum away" after hitting him with these. By this I mean go aloof for a while or make him wait an extra day to see you.

Another option is to add a neg, for instance:

You: "Your blue eyes were driving me wild last night...If only they were green!"

This gives him the compliment but pulls it back in an instant. This leaves him confused about how you feel and a confused man is a man that wants the answer...all good!

3. The "Tease" text.

You: "Panties? I wore none last night"

You: "Hmm, I wonder if things could crazy between us"

You: "I thought about you last night...late last night"

You: "I'm sleeping naked tonight"

You: "Next weekend, maybe I'll wear something special for you"

You: "I brought you into my fantasy last night"

What makes these so powerful is what you DON'T say and this is the holy grail of texting. Always text less than him; get his mind thinking of you and you will hold the cards when you get together.

I love these gems! They are powerful. How do I know? I've asked thousands of men on my website and they **tell me** this stuff works. They don't want to hear, "How was your f**** dumb ass day?" or "Whatcha f**** doing?" (Sorry, I got a bit emotional there! But then, I hate these kinds of texts.)

Change my texts above to work for your situation

or copy them straight out **then** watch your results. Are some a bit slutty? Yes! But this is the whole idea. You are **teasing** him, not actually doing anything (yet!) Yes, it's a game but that's **okay** because you just met and you **need** to stir the pot.

CHAPTER 1:

Tension and Attraction in Texting Made Simple

I swear...there's something about you ladies. You know instinctively how to turn on the charm. The looks you give us, the tone of voice you use, everything comes together when you want it to. Within an instant you can turn a man's heart and head to complete mush!

I know all of you can turn the charm when you're faced with a man you're attracted to. You know how to dress, how to walk, how to smile coyly and yet, with texting, suddenly all of these assets go out the window. You're staring at a little blank screen on your Droid and you're saying to yourself "how in the hell am I going to be cute and flirty on this dinky little phone?!"

You get confused, you may even get a bit nervous. You start shooting from the hip, not knowing whether your texts are hitting their target or not. For all you know your text just hit an innocent bystander. More often than not you hit yourself!

The frustration is completely natural. You gals evolved your flirting skills over millions of years. Whether you know it or not flirting comes as natural to you as flight comes to a bird. You're used to face-to-face contact, yet when someone hands you a phone and says "type" you're simply not in your element.

But we're going to change that.

In chapter one, we're going to hit the topic of building tension (aka flirting) hard and fast. We're going to briefly go over the psychology of it, and then, with plenty of examples, I'm going to show you how to take your text flirting to the next level.

Catch Me If You Can

Now, you could keep reading this chapter until you memorize it, but if you want a short cut I'll be happy to provide you one. That above phrase, "catch me if you can" is all you need to know about a great flirty text.

What it comes down to is this: all you need to create tension is to stay a step ahead of your man **at all times**.

Staying ahead of him helps build attraction. Attraction is created from two things:

a. Because a person is not entirely available.

b. Because that person has something that you don't have.

In terms of availability, the most common way to create a sense of being unavailable is to tease, which helps set boundaries but also increases expectations. You put ideas in our heads of what **could** happen and what you **might** do. This is the essence and the core of flirting.

> Him: I've got a ticket to the hockey game with your name on it!

> *You: One ticket? At least get two so I can invite a girl-friend of mine!*

> Him: ha! So that's a yes?

> *You: Hmm, only if you wear those jeans with the holes in them. You know, the ones that show some skin?*

His mind is likely in overdrive at this point, and it's all because you teased and mentioned that you liked seeing his legs through a few holes in his jeans. Men feel alive when women provoke them with little comments like that.

With regards to B, tension and attraction can be built because we adore and even envy a person's skill or expertise. We are also attracted to the fact the other people find that person attractive. It's for this reason that famous people are constantly marrying other famous people. They need their partner to be adored as much as they are, or else the balance gets shifted and contempt slowly seeps in.

An important aspect about both of these is that a balance must be shared in regards to value and tension.

There is a back-and-forth element to attraction, and for that to work you must find a partner that can create tension in a way similar to your own. More on that later; for now, just know that you must be able to convey a sense of value in order to find men of value. You must bring your own strengths to the table if you want a man with his own attractive strengths.

Your goal then is to develop a sense of yourself that you are confident of. Confidence is one of the most important tools to create tension. Without it, you're constantly falling into a trap where your worth is created by the man you're with. I talk more about this in my book *The Social Tigress*, which I highly recommend if you want to really delve into the psychological aspects of maintaining a relationship!

Bitch Power

Why are men more often attracted to the bitchy girls over nice ones? Hint: it's the same reason why you ladies are attracted to bad boys.

Bitches are all about being bold and edgy. They taunt men, they egg men on, they keep men at the edge of their seat. All together, they make for extremely attractive partners!

> Him: Hitting the bars with a few friends tonight. Care to join?

You: Liar. You don't have friends.

Him: I bought a few last weekend. Hopefully I got a good deal.

Taken by itself, that could be seen as a mean comment. A bitchy comment! But if it's handled with poise, it can be an amazing flirting tool. Men (the good ones, the ones with thick skins) love when women use this in casual conversation, and you ladies are equally challenged when your men do it to you.

And let's be honest here: you don't want someone boring, some "yes dear" man who slavers over you and does your bidding. Sometimes that's exactly what men imagine you want, but if we actually did that you'd lose all attraction for us.

A quote by Oscar Wilde sums this up nicely. "Women tend to find men irretrievably bad, and leave them unattractively good." To my ears, that sounds just about right!

So, unleash the inner bitch!

Him: How's your day going?

You: My vibe burned out...online ordering a new one :-)

Him: Hahaha...well, maybe I can help?

You: No response
(ouch! This guy's balls are in a vice after this one!)

Bitches and dicks are great partners, at least at first, because we are attracted to their confidence, their bravado or their sassiness. Be wary, however, of contempt seeping in. If you are not an equal force in the relationship (if you aren't playing your part as a hardcore bitch!) then this can quickly occur, spoiling the relationship forever by creating a negative tension.

"Hey, Gregg, I'm not so sure. Isn't any kind of tension bad for a relationship? Don't you want to be in harmony with your partner?"

No, no, and no. **Harmony is boring!** You want engagement, aggression, passion! You want tension! Now, as I said above, some tension can be negative, and is made so by the balance being jolted out of proportions. If a relationship is full of this kind of contempt, it simply cannot last, and it's best to simply move on. But good tension is what makes great relationships last. It's the challenge that I was talking about, that amazing thing that allows two people to grow together.

Above I gave you an example of a sassy text, but how do you temper something that you want to be perceived as sassy and not downright mean? On a little text screen, it isn't always easy to express sarcasm. But that's why they invented smiley faces!

You: I ate way too much at dinner last night. I'm still sick!

Him: I know! I remember turning my back for a second and you had eaten everything on my plate!

> *You: Shush, last time I checked you had a bit of a pudge yourself! :-)*

Without the smiley face, that comment could have been taken the wrong way. The exclamation mark helps add a bit of sarcasm, but the smiley face ensures that he knows you're not demeaning his gut.

There's plenty more to talk about in regards to emoticons (aka smiley faces and such) as well as "dampeners" as I like to call them, or ways to keep a conversation light. Some of these are good, others are actually pitfalls that can damage you more than help you. All of that in due time though! For now, let's move onto some great tips on how to build tension in text form.

Some Tips for Building Tension

This segment has a number of great tips for making that tension happen in a text, but if I could pick one that I feel is the most important, it would be this:

Ladies, YOU set the "hidden" tempo of the relationship.

What do I mean by hidden? I mean that while a man is expected to be assertive, it's not necessarily because you aren't so yourself. **It's because you let him be.** You know it's important to him to take charge and you know that if you let him catch you too early, the relationship isn't likely to fully bloom. It is therefore up to you, ladies, to set the true tempo of the relationship. You're in charge of the speed from first date to engagement.

Ever heard of the saying "a man chases a woman until she catches him?" It's a truism that isn't going away anytime soon!

Of course, all of us can get impatient, and maybe you're frustrated that you have to play such a game at all. But this is wishful thinking and far from reality. You know it already: a man will jump right in. He doesn't care! He wants you right now, from the minute he sets eyes on you. Sure you could give it all to him right away, but if you do, the gig is up. You don't realize it, but 9 times out of 10, you just lost the boy.

Let's take a look at a few other tension-building tips!

The Sound of Silence

It's not just a great song from Simon and Garfunkel, it's important if you hope to create tension through texting! Silence is a powerful tool and can be used to gain the upper hand in the tension game. Think less is more. Think enhancing mystery. This is where texting can totally win out against the phone. It may be that in a phone call you'll say too much. With a text, you can be very specific about what you say, and what you don't say.

From this, an essential takeaway: the person who texts last is the less mysterious one. If you don't respond, if you don't comment, you automatically gain the upper hand.

Him: Hey, did I just see you at the mall?

> You: *Nope, that was my evil twin, she's buying naughty lingerie as usual.*

> Him: Lol, I'm not so sure if that was your twin!

> You: *Radio silence*

Bam! You just knocked this out of the park! I won't even comment on the sassy (and sexy) response to his question, but the fact that you left him hanging after his second response makes him want you even more. Guarantee he's sitting there hoping, no, praying that you text him back. But you're not going to because you know better!

Remember: it's about perceiving to care less. It doesn't necessarily mean you care less, in fact you might love the guy like crazy. But you must give the impression that you are relaxed about it, or you'll quickly find yourself caught (or worse, chasing after him!)

Destroy Boredom, Shatter All Things Conventional!

> You: *So, what's going on with you these days?*

> Him: Not a lot. Just working, going to school.

I'm going to stop here. I wanted to make that a long text conversation, but I felt repulsed by where it was going. You do know where it's going right? To the relationship graveyard! It's going nowhere. There's nothing in that first comment that added any value at all to the conversation.

Two huge mistakes were played out here. First, tension is simply not created by asking general questions. How was your day? What are you doing right now? What's the weather like? No, no and no. These are tension killers is what they are, and if you want to keep yourself sounding fun and fresh you won't be using these general questions to start a texting convo.

Second problem: nobody wants to answer a question like that in a text. Even if you have the most easy-to-use handheld on the planet, you're going to get sick of typing out a response the size of Moby Dick really fast. Keep it simple and stick with precise questions that your boy can answer without too much trouble.

You want short, fun and challenging interactions. You want to go bold, quirky, jokey, fun and direct! Forget the boring stuff and show him your flirty side. You have tons of time to figure out a response, so relax and wait for it to come to you!

You: How was your chemistry class? Inhale any asbestos in the lab?

Him: Sure did. Court dates set for tomorrow!

There we go! Much more focused, and you added in a bit of cheek as well.

Stick with the Mysterious, Avoid the Vague!

Mysterious is always good. The more you can get him wondering about what you're doing, the better. Mystery is invoked by staying partly aloof. You want him thinking that you're busy doing lots of fun things, or maybe seeing other interesting people!

Him: What are you up to this weekend beau?

You: Ugh...tons of 100 pound text books to read. Might have to skip dance on Sat.

See what you just did there? You created mystery by avoiding some boring comment like "Not sure, what are you doing?" You're obviously busy, and by the sound of it you're meeting people that are NOT him at that dance class. Trust me, he's going to see you as a serious challenge, adding to the attraction.

Responses like these, however, are completely unacceptable:

- "Well, let's hang out in a few days."

- "Cool, talk to you later."

- "Bored. What's up?"

Similarly, keep ugly vague words out of your text box. Maybe, kind of, perhaps, sort of, all trash, all vague! Stick to language that's alive and bold, and you'll become a master texter in no time.

Give Him Content to Work With. Be a Flirt!

Challenge, challenge, challenge! This is your goal when you're sending over those texts. You want to give him something that he **wants** to respond to. In most cases this is because you teased him or mentioned something that he loves talking about.

> *You: It was great meeting your parents last night. Your father is an attractive man! Think he's available?*

> Him: Just wait 25 years and I'll introduce you to his twin. In the mean time you're stuck with me.

> *You: Drat! I hate long waits!*

Think of little comments that will egg him on. You want keep poking and prodding him. Get him smiling or even laughing and he will love you for it!

> *You: My girlfriend is in town and wants to meet you. Think I might have convinced her to do a three-some. You down?*

> Him: Huh?! Seriously?!

> *You: No, that was a joke you dirty boy. Or was it?*

And of course, if you want his blood boiling, you can pull the jealousy card. Of course, you'll want to do this in a measured way, otherwise it could easily backfire. Some guys are going to react to it differently than others. If you've got a Klingon in your life, I'd suggest you stay clear of anything related to jealousy, even in jest.

Here's a great example where it worked:

> *You: Well crap. I have to hit the gym and check out all those buff studs again. B.O.R.I.N.G.*

> Him: Five dollars says I can beat any of them at arm wrestling...or at least HALO.

> *You: lol...ok, if you don't hear from me, I took a stud home!*

The thing that makes it okay to do is the **obvious** humor. The B.O.R.I.N.G comment as well as the outright, blatant mention that you would be staring at guys with big muscles is a dead giveaway (or so he thinks) that you aren't interested in doing so (or at least not interested in them on a dating level.) But then you turn it around and make him jealous when you say your last line...powerful stuff!

That about concludes Chapter 1. My hope is that you have a lot of great examples to get inspiration from, as well as a few core rules that aren't just going to see you through the texting world, but your dating life in general. Remember that texting has and always will be an ease of use tool to relay a message quickly and effectively, and that is still its primary purpose. But for quick little flirt sessions, no technology is better than an SMS text message.

CHAPTER 2:

Setting Boundaries, Building Respect

Welcome back! You've made it to chapter two, and by now you're capable of knocking a guy's socks off with your deviously flirty text messages. That's a damned good skill to have, but you'll need other skills if you want to turn those first few dates into a long-term relationship.

Equally important to tension is that not-so-little thing we call respect. Respect tends to be sorely lacking in many relationships, and without it no relationship can thrive. We're knocking out the hard-hitting facts behind building respect in the first section of this chapter. By the time you're finished reading this you'll understand the why and how of creating boundaries in a medium as simple as a tiny text message.

R.E.S.P.E.C.T.

You know it's important. You know that a relationship isn't going to last without it. What you may not know is

why it's essential to maintaining your connection with that special person. More importantly, you may not be sure **how** you can promote its growth.

Boundaries, first of all, are created out of respect for **ourselves** first. That is the origin of all boundaries we create. No woman who loves herself will allow someone else to dictate everything she does, or let someone have a say in everywhere she goes. Without these boundaries, certain unscrupulous men will trample upon their women, which can quickly turn into an abusive relationship.

Not all men will take it that far of course. However, most men will quickly lose interest in a woman who has few or no boundaries. The reason, of course, is that men need a challenge. They need to feel they earned you: that they fought for you and won. At the core of this is value: all men want a woman that has things going for her. In this sense, both men and women are similar; we just express it in different ways.

Read the conversation below and ask yourself why this woman is not respecting herself, and thus not setting boundaries:

Him: Hey what's up? You doing anything tonight?

Her: No, just chillaxing. How about you?

Him: Let's do dinner. Six sound good?

Her: Sure, see you at six!

Some of you are probably thinking nothing is wrong here. She was excited! She wasn't doing anything, so why not go out with him?

But here we come to a dilemma. While it may be nice to see him, something just happened during that text conversation which detracted from this woman's value (and thus how attractive she appears to him). This woman mentioned immediately that she was completely free, and then accepted an offer for a date just a few hours beforehand.

On the surface, that seems like a minor issue. In reality however this has brought a new status quo into the relationship, where he can call her up and ask her to hang out with him anytime he wants.

It doesn't matter if she was doing something or not. What matters is that she should value herself and her time enough to set a boundary, to let him know that she isn't at his beck and call. This reinforces your value, which in turn makes him more attracted to you, not less. It is a mistake to think that he will go looking for someone else if you say no. And if he does, maybe he's not the guy you thought he was.

Let's solve the issue and rewrite our example:

Him: Hey Susie! How about Chinese tonight? I'm buying!

Susie: Hey! I'd love to, but this is really short notice. Can we rain check? How about Sat?

> Him: Yeah, sorry. Of course! I'll call you on Saturday
> then. =)

Much better! And what's great about this is that you did it in a friendly way. See, you don't need to be hurtful when you say no. The use of "hey" with an exclamation point at the start makes you sound excited to hear from him, and you ask him for a rain check instead of just demanding one. You didn't get angry, you still sound upbeat and you didn't hurt his feelings. And as an added bonus, you set a definitive date (Saturday) and you didn't text him back after his second message (adding to your mystery!) Well done!

It's Never Too Early to Start Building Respect

The above text conversation may have been different between two people that have been dating for some time, when things relax a bit and you have a better understanding of each other's value. When you just meet a guy however, it's never too early to start building respect. The sooner you set those boundaries, the better chances you have of keeping the relationship strong.

How do you begin setting boundaries? Well, the best way, perhaps the only real way, is to create a life of value for yourself outside of your relationships with men. That could be work, school, volunteering, hobbies and pastimes. It could be something as simple as a cooking class, or a weekly hike with friends, or a wine-tasting group on the weekends. When you do this, you prove to him that you are challenging yourself, and that in turn makes him desire you more.

This kind of lifestyle **automatically** creates boundaries for you. If he wants to go out on Tuesday, and you've got a class on Tuesday, you simply aren't free, and a boundary is set. He begins to appreciate that you have a life outside of his and his desire to have you skyrockets!

The Power of the Sex Card

Those first few days of a relationship are crucial for respect building. Especially in the beginning, it is you ladies who hold the power of the sex card. Men can't hold this card: if given the chance 90 percent of them would have sex with you the minute they met you. If you play this card correctly, you are guaranteed to drastically increase his interest for you. If you play it too soon, you've proven that you don't have much of a boundary regarding who you give yourself too, and how soon.

For the same reasons, constant texts with sexual innuendos begin to sound trashy almost immediately. Good men, men that you **want** to date, are quickly going to realize that you're not being sexy, but insecure. I'll get into this topic more later on, but with regards to sexting and sending nude pictures of yourself, my advice is: **just don't do it!** It's not only a terrible way to maintain a relationship, but it could do serious damage to your character if the wrong person gets ahold of them.

Resist Seeking Approval

Boundaries are incredibly useful because they can help us resist the urge to bend to someone else's will. They form the framework which allows us to create strong and long lasting relationships. For that reason, it's extremely important that we have these rules in place **before** we get ourselves involved in one new relationship after another.

Boundaries are signals that only confident people can produce. People that can say "no" and stand firm are attractive to us. At the end of the day, who are you going to go to if you are seeking approval: someone weak and unsure of themselves, or someone confident with a foundation of strong boundaries? That confident person's approval means much more to us.

You must develop this foundation if you want a healthy relationship. By maintaining boundaries, you show that you don't need to seek that other person's approval. Eventually this can even change how attracted you are to certain men. You may find that the person you used to love is less valuable than you first imagined.

The Takeaway

Before I move on, I want you to make sure you have these points down pat:

- You make yourself valuable by not always being available. Women who bend over backward to please a man are unknowingly killing their chances at a relationship.

- Stay away from sexting and nude pictures. This gets him wanting you but in all the wrong ways.

- Love yourself first, and only then find a man to love. You simply cannot sacrifice self-respect out of a need to be liked by someone. It is not the fix you imagine it to be!

As a final piece of advice, you simply cannot live your life worrying that "that special guy" is going to slip out of your life if you don't make some concessions to your boundaries. Ladies, you **must** be willing to defend your values if you are to have any value in the eyes of your man. If your values end up making a man turn away and leave, you need to realize that he's not the guy you imagine him to be. Either you are incompatible or he is really on the lookout for a woman that he can control.

I know you don't want that. Show your pride and stick to your values! Millions of guys are out there, and by sticking to your convictions you leave yourself open to find someone even better.

Bringing it All Together: Building Respect through Texting

Now to the fun part! Let's go over the different ways that you can create respect and promote boundaries with a few simple texting examples.

Example: Know Your Role!

Smart men and women who play the dating game right

know how to really maximize their role in the relationship. They have a sense of what they do best, and they play those cards to their full advantage.

Let's go beyond modern feminism and political correctness here and get serious: men and women aren't playing the same roles in dating. The man needs to play his part and take charge, at least outwardly. The woman, meanwhile, does her part by promoting that interest, by leading the man forward without actually taking charge herself.

"A man chases a woman until she catches him." That age old saying still has great weight and meaning in an age where both sexes are constantly confused over what roles they should be playing.

Now, I know plenty of you ladies aren't interested in being patient. You want to pounce! The bad news is it isn't always the smartest move to be the one asking him out on dates; in fact, it can be damaging, potentially confusing him and weakening his position in the relationship. So instead of outright telling him you want a date, you're going to do this much more subtly. The good news is you can do this without much trouble!

You: Read this movie review and tell me what you think (link review)

Him: Actually looks awesome. Didn't know it had come out yet!

You: Sure has...and since we both want to see it we may as well just go together!

Him: haha...we sure can. How about Saturday, we'll make it dinner and a movie?

You: You got it mister!

What does this conversation do? Well, it's playful for one. You start off with a challenge (you want him to read a review and then have him express his opinion), and then you reasonably suggest that because you both want to see it, you "may as well just go together." Now, **of course** you want to go specifically with him, but you downplay that fact in a teasing way. Finally, the use of "mister" is another cute tease that you can use. More on nicknames later on!

Men **love** when women do this. You playfully sprung a date on us, you acted in a way that was fun and exciting, and if he is **at all** interested in you he is going to go on that date with you!

Turn the date into his idea. If you want to go on a date, construct a conversation in a way that makes it seem like it's his idea!

You: Just got back from a Chinese buffet with my mom. Kick me if I ever mention going again.

Him: Yikes! Was it that bad?

You: It was! The taste is still in my mouth! Quick, what's the opposite of Chinese food?

Him: I'm going with American food. Final answer.

You: Good, I'm with you! Thursday after classes?

Him: haha, you bet!

Again, playful, fun, and witty—no man is going to say no to this!

So I'm giving you a proposed goal: act relaxed, be playful, and these kinds of conversations will come. Don't try to write some template with set responses. He may respond in a way that you can't work in a date. Don't worry! There are other opportunities, and if you are having fun little conversations like this, an opportunity will come up. I promise!

Remember: let the guy work his alpha stuff. It's easy in our day and age for a woman to forget her subtlety and patience and just make a show of being the "man" of the relationship. But as I mentioned above, it doesn't always pay dividends, and could end up killing the relationship.

Example: Of Course You're Not Sorry!

We are constantly testing each other's boundaries, and that's a good thing! If we didn't we would never be able to tell whether someone is good for us or not.

However there is one thing that couples tend to do

that simply doesn't look good in a text, and that is apologize for a perceived mistake. If you really screwed up and need to apologize, you either need to do it face to face or call. However, for all texting related matters, apologizing is rarely warranted.

>*You: Going to John's Pub tonight w/ friends. Where are you heading?*

>Him: Probably Dirt Bags. Not sure though.

>*You: Dirt Bags! What a dump!*

>Him: Hey, I happen to like it!

>*You: Really? Sorry, didn't know.*

Stop right there. This final comment from you, this apology, may seem like the right thing to do, but it's a bad idea. It spoils any additional fun you could have in the conversation. Worse, it's actually a conversation ender. What is he going to say? "It's okay?" "No problem?" You can't come back from it.

But let's look at it again and see what we can do to fix it!

>*You: Dirt Bags! What a dump!*

>Him: Hey, I happen to like it!

> You: I'm just saying...it takes a lot of preparation to go there. You have to avoid a shower for like...a week or something!

> Him: I'll avoid showers for a month if I can get my hands on $1 beers!

> You: Well trust me, the day they offer $1 wine coolers I'll never shower again either.

Bam! You manage to keep the conversation going in a fun way, and you made it light enough to where he felt like he could joke about it. That's the power of flirty, witty dialogue: it works to both to build tension **and** to test boundaries. Maybe you won't go to his bar and maybe he won't go to yours, but that's okay because you can find other venues that you both agree on, and you are both more attracted to each other because neither one of you caved.

You are an attractive, intelligent woman. More important, you are your own woman. You don't **need** to do whatever it is he wants to do. Set your boundaries, all while finding fun ways to test his. If you can do this, you set the stage for an amazing and exciting relationship!

CHAPTER 3:

NEED
The Black Hole of Relationships

Sometimes we can be our own worst enemies. Our attempts to express ourselves backfire; we are so intent upon getting what it is we want that we end up pushing it away. That, in a nutshell, is the danger of need. It's a relationship destroyer, a leech that will suck the attraction and respect right out of a couple's life, and oftentimes it's not something you can recover from.

Whether you knew it or not, many of you have released the Great Need Vampire on some unsuspecting guy, and some of you have also had a boyfriend sic that very same vampire on you as well. I suspect that at some point or another we've all encountered it. The relationship quickly becomes unstable, the balance tilts too far in one direction or another, and things fall apart.

Take a look at this text conversation and ask yourself where this girl goes wrong:

Jake: Hey Kim. Slammed at work this week. Can we rain check our date on Tuesday?

Kim: Oh c'mon. You've got a better excuse than that I'm sure!

Jake: Uh. No. I'm slammed at work.

Kim: Whatever. It's fine.

Jake: No response

Kim: K. Don't respond then.

Kim sounds...well, she sounds uninterested in an obviously needy way. To this guy, who let's say she met a month ago, she is giving off obvious signs of a Klingon. Kim has a stronger likelihood of being abducted by aliens than she does of getting back with this guy. The damage has been done.

These are not responses from a woman that doesn't care. On the contrary, she is way **too** interested in him, and in an attempt to legitimize herself and have him love her back she goes too far and destroys the balance. Her first response was likely written not because she really thought he was lying, but because she thought he **should** want to spend more time with her, and that he **should** be doing whatever it takes to be with her.

Perhaps unknowingly, perhaps out of a sense of expectations, she just sabotaged her own future with this

guy that she liked. This is not an exaggerated conversation. Most of us have either done something similar to
this, or been on the receiving end of it.

Final note: we all make assumptions. But you need to
keep your emotions in check and assume he is telling the
truth until it's proven otherwise.

It Goes Beyond the First Few Dates

You gals know how ugly need appears during those first
few months of dating. But need irrevocably alters any
relationship that it enters into. Marriages fall apart because need shifts the balance and creates an unassailable
divide between two people. What I'm saying is that it's
not just advice you want to follow for the first few weeks.
Need is something you need to be careful of for the rest
of your days, in sickness and in health, till death do you
part, and anywhere in between!

I don't mean you can't find comfort in somebody. Having someone you can go to when times get tough is what
relationships are all about. But when bitterness gets added into the equation because of some nagging doubt you
have about his commitment to you, **that's** when things
take a bad turn.

Controlling the Urge

We've all had the urge to blurt out our worst fears to
our partners. It's something we can't help but consider,

especially when some nagging doubt is whispering in our ear. But you must learn to control that voice if you want to keep that amazing relationship you have.

It's our desire to seek approval of that person that we love that makes it so difficult. EVERYONE feels this need from time to time. But if you're always seeking your man's approval, any attraction he has for you is going to go out the window. It comes down, once again, to challenge. If you're seeking approval from rather than challenging your man, your value takes a hit and the balance shifts against you.

Don't go there! No matter how desperately in love you are, you must remain in control of yourself and your fears. Having a strong emotional fortitude is a desirable thing to have in a partner. You want to know that the person you're dating isn't going to fall apart at the drop of a hat.

Which is why as a dating coach I'm **constantly** telling my clients to stay busy! Build a life for yourself that you love and feel great about. It is the only way I know that will keep that urge to seek approval down to a reasonable level. Because when you realize that you yourself are valuable, you feel less of a need to draw that value from other places (aka your man).

Let's look at a few false roads that people are always going down in a relationship. While they may seem like approaches that will put your man in his place, they are actually relationship enders that at best will create contempt in your partner, and at worst end the relationship outright.

Unfortunately, women tend to hit men with this stuff via some really ugly text messages because they are simply too uncomfortable with talking about it to his face. But these kinds of conversations, if they merit a conversation at all (almost never!) you **need to have them face to face**. How in the world could you express these kinds of deep unsatisfied longings in fifty words or less? Most of us couldn't do it if we had all day!

Relationship Killer #1: Guilt Tripping

Guilt tripping seems to be some kind of last resort, used to bring back your man from the edge of the precipice. It's like throwing a collar around a dog's neck just before the dog goes off a cliff.

Outcome: The dog is strangled and you're in the same position regardless.

If you've come to a point where you have to guilt trip a guy to get him to do what you want, you need to take a step back and realize that you're just killing off the relationship in a different way.

You: What's up? What are you doing tonight?

Him: Going out with a few buddies to O'Malley's Bar!

You: Sounds like fun. Maybe an invite next time?

Him: Sure

You: Just seems like you hang out with them a lot is all.

Congrats. This is going to be something he shares with his buddies for the foreseeable future. And to be honest, you would deserve it!

There's nothing subtle about how insecure this is. You are putting your fears into text form and displaying them blatantly to this guy you may or may not have just met. Either way, showing this kind of weakness is one of the most unattractive things you could do. It adds to his perception of you as someone undesirable, someone not confident.

A guy responds to guilt in pretty much the opposite way you'd like him to. He will clam up, stonewall, and do everything but the thing you want him to do. Even if he does do it, he will hold a grudge about it.

If your guy is starting to feel distant, you have a much better chance of getting him back by **ignoring** him than you do guilting him into coming back to you. Stay aloof and start dating around a bit. If he does come back, it's because you've suddenly grown more attractive by being suddenly out of reach.

Relationship Killer #2: Showing Obvious Desperation

I want you to give these texts a good, hard look, and then swear to me you'll never say them or anything like them to a man ever again!

- "Hey, I feel like you're being distant lately."

- "Why don't we hang out as much as we used to?"

- "Should I just assume you're seeing someone else at this point?"

- "Why don't you try asking me out sometime?"

These kinds of texts are how you get blacklisted from a guy straight away. They reek of desperation, they display a woman that is trying to push and prod and otherwise force a guy into feeling something they may not feel yet. Ladies, if you find yourself **pushing** a guy in any way to show his love for you, it's going to send him running. Do your part by staying away from such desperate quotes, and start thinking about ways that you can get **him** chasing **you**.

Relationship Killer #3: He Pulls Away & You Give Chase

Both men and women are guilty of this. They realize the person they like is getting more distant, and instead of doing what they should do (give them space, stay rather unavailable yourself) they overcorrect and start asking very unattractive questions like "what did I do wrong" or "how can I win you back."

Resist these at all costs! As a woman, you're texts must invoke the language of charm and flirtation. If you see him pulling away, you still have a few cards up your sleeve that don't involve running to him and begging to get him back.

You: Pretty sure I just talked to your ex at Frank's Bar.

Him: lol BS...wait which one?

You: You player! She didn't give me a name, just a number.

Him: If it's number 53 tell her she owes me money.

In this instance, you hooked him immediately with your first comment. He immediately wants to know what his ex is saying about him to the girl he's been hanging out with, even if his interest in you is starting to waver a bit. Given, he may or may not come back at you with some humor. Many times he will demand to know what she said. In this case, play it cool and mention only vague comments like "well...let's just say we have a lot in common!" or "she had some fun things to say about you!" :-)

If your guy seems to have fallen into obscurity, it may be because you were tightening the noose a little too early. If you've sent a text or two and he hasn't responded, your best bet is to wait a week (or longer!) and then start up a new conversation with him in an attempt at a refresh. Whatever you make that fresh conversation about, make sure it's **fun** and not "where have you been this last week."
Things you might say:

- "You ever been to X restaurant? I just had this burger that tasted like toe jam. Stay away!"

- "What's up stud? Was just admiring Justin Beiber's skinny biceps and immediately thought of you!"

- "I think I got Herpes from just looking at Miley Cyrus's tongue at the VMAs last night."

All of these work for different reasons, but the main take away is that you stay away from anything that isn't light and friendly. You want to be fun and flirty and exciting, since that's the only way he's going to respond back. Make your text to him **worthy** of a response! In all of these you were flirty and friendly. If he laughed, then you have him hooked, and there's a strong likelihood that he will text back.

If he doesn't text back, your only chance may be to cease all contact with him and move on. That may sound cruel and depressing, but at this point you simply aren't connecting with him and there's likely nothing you could say to him that would entice his flagging interest in you.

If you're having trouble thinking of something, look for things that you had in common and comment on that in some way. Or, like the last example, look for current events that he likely saw and find something funny to say about them.

Finishing Up Chapter 3

A brief chapter, but a very important one. Since expressing too much need is probably the biggest reason why balance becomes skewed, it was critical that I shed some light on the subject in our eBook here. After reading Chapter 3, you ladies are more than capable of avoiding most forms of need (at least the bad kinds!) All it takes is a bit of effort on your part to develop your own confidence and sense of worth.

Because the truth is, trying to achieve your own value from the man you're with is going to destroy your chances of a great future relationship.

CHAPTER 4:

Gregg's Top Ten Texting Blunders

Ah yes, the chapter you've all been waiting for! Texting may be an amazing platform for flirting and building respect, but this chapter is dedicated to all the ways in which that very same platform can go horribly wrong. Indeed, messing around with any one of these no-no's is the fastest way to get the door slammed in your face.

In my top ten, I go over everything from excessive emoticons to drunk-texting your man at 3 in the morning. For many of you ladies it's going to be a wakeup call. If you ever catch yourself doing any of my ten blunders, I want you to stick your head in your freezer and cool off for a bit! Yes, they're that serious.

Let's get started shall we? Starting with Number 10!

Fail #10: You're Not Varying the Timings of Your Texts
You've read the rules of texting. There's an etiquette that's in place and you do your very best to follow it. But in siding

too closely with the rules, you've unknowingly turned into a rigid automaton, texting him at the same time each day, waiting for that 3 PM mark to hit so you can press send!

Or maybe you think 3 PM is a dead giveaway to him that you're sitting there by your phone trying to figure out when to text him. So you wait until 3:03 to make it seem more natural. But then, you're missing the whole point!

You want to space your responses out in random intervals. That way he never knows when to expect a response. He sees you as an engaged, busy person—so busy in fact, that you simply can't get around to texting him on some days!

Let's say you are so excited about seeing a text from him, you go ahead and shoot him a text back immediately. But you need to think that over. Immediately sending a response can be a bit...off-putting. It makes it seem like you're sitting there, phone at the ready, prepared to give a response to him whether you're busy or not. Sound a bit creepy? That's because it is!

So follow a little rule: If he takes five minutes, you take five minutes. Or better yet, increase it to ten minutes. You want to be just **slightly** less interested than he is. This is when being chased comes into play. Remember, you can't be the one texting him more often. It's his job to be doing that to you!

Funny story. I find this particular rule to be incredibly powerful. Not too long ago I taught the same principle to this sassy young thing that I've been dating, and now, get this: **she's using it against me, The Dating Master!** Even worse…**I love it!** She is making me want her more simply because she is being a Scrooge when it comes to her texts.

You withhold them, and guys will love you all the more for it.

Fail # 9: The Infamous Drunk Text

If you don't fire off texts when you're drunk, you definitely know someone who does. Usually this poor individual gets into some serious trouble, or at best makes a complete fool out of herself or himself.

The really disastrous emotions come out when we're drunk. We tend to express those fears, those desires, and those regrets much more openly, and when you add texting into the mix it gets even worse. If you've been dying to text this boy for a while, and you're downright shit-faced, **give your phone to a friend.** It could very well save your fledgling relationship with your new guy.

Even if your guy comes out with you, you're going to be drunker than he is. Worse, you could do something with him that (soberly speaking) you're not ready to do yet. Chances are he will take you up on it, but if that's the case his respect for you may have just tanked.

Fail #8:
You're Talking to Him Like He's One of Your Girlfriends

You: New manicure! I'm so excited!

Him: You know I love well-manicured women!

You: Sure do...and later on I'm going to Macy's for their 50% off scarf sale!

Him: You know I love women in scarves!

You: I sure do!

I'm going to throw it out there: this is unacceptable. In this example the guy is seemingly showing some interest in your affairs, but in reality he is looking at the phone as if it just grew legs and pincers.

Talk to your girlfriends about this kind of stuff! Guys love it when girls look good, but we usually aren't interested in how you got there. If it takes you three hours to get ready, we don't want to see it. We are just happy that it happened. Call us heartless if you want, but it's not something that we can readily change about our characters.

Remember: even if he **seems** interested, in all likelihood he's not!

Fail #7: You Text Like a 13 Year Old

If you're reading this, I like to think you're old enough to drive a car. And if you're old enough to drive a car, you're waaaaaaay over the kind of chatter that you see on the phone of a 13 year old girl.

Girlfriend: Lulz that guy was digging u!

You (when you were 13): OMG ya wut a qt!!!

Girlfriend: SRSLY! BTW wut u doin 2nite? U goin 2 see Brad Pitts new movie?

You: Hellz ya! It looks totz swt!

Huh? What?! Oh God, I can't do it anymore. I gave it my best shot to write like that but I felt a stroke coming on. My point with that conversation is simple: it looks like trash! It looks like something a high school girl would write. If you're sending this kind of tripe to a guy, he's going to laugh in your face.

Apply standard grammar rules (pretty please?) Spell each word correctly, or at least phonetically! This is really the only way you can ensure that he takes you seriously. Given, you can write out some acronyms (lol is so commonplace that you can use it without fear of being ridiculed), just don't overuse them to death.

Fail #6: You Sent Nude Pictures of Yourself

Go ahead: find a search engine and type in "ex girlfriends nude pics." You'll find a number of sites dedicated to uploading pictures of women that were far, far too trusting. Once the picture is on the internet, the damage is done. You may break up with your ex and never know that he did such a thing to you. It could be up forever. You could be running as the first female president of the United States and have someone stumble upon it.

Even if you're not running for political office, you don't want to have something like that on the web. The best way to avoid problems like this is to never give the guy a chance to post it! Don't send stuff like this EVER. It could come back and bite you in ways you cannot fathom.

Yes, it's tempting to add a bit of sexting appeal to a relationship. You want his blood boiling; you want him thinking about you. But as I've shown you throughout the book, there are ways you can do so without taking a snap shot of your Brazilian wax job. The only thing you're flirting with in that instance is danger!

Stick with words. Or, if you want to send him something, send him a picture of some cleavage, or your butt in some tight jeans. Honest to God that is even more attractive to us, since it leaves more to the imagination, which is 90% of sex appeal in the first place.

Fail #5: Your Responses Lead Nowhere

I feel for you gals, I really do. You all must be the ones that set the tempo of the relationship, and that can be difficult. It's hard to know when you should tempt him with a possible date, or how long you should space your responses. It's not easy! But trust me, we love you for it!

One mistake I constantly see is women sending texts that are like roads to nowhere. Let's say you like a guy but you're unsure how to proceed in a text conversation. Perhaps he's trying to ask you out, but you're busy that night and can't make it happen:

Jack: Hey, so how about Saturday night? I'll pick you up at 8?

You: Can't do it Saturday

Jack: Ah, no problem. Maybe Sunday?

You: It's a crazy weekend. I wish I could but I'm swamped!

Jack: haha...that's okay! We'll set something up later on then.

Maybe you really **are** busy, and that would be a good thing in developing your sense of value to him. But your brief responses are being taken by Jack as an obvious sign that you're not interested. If I received this kind of message I'd be on to the next date with someone else.

The fix is easy. He has invited you on a date, he set the time and it didn't work out for you. So... **give him a time that works.** Set something specific. "This weekend is crazy, but I'd love to see you. You up for dinner during the week? Maybe Tuesday, same time?" Even if he is not available, he will take that as a sign that you still want to see him. It's a critical step and if you ignore it, you may miss out on a great guy. There's a fine line between being aloof (which is good) and acting like you truly aren't interested to him (this is bad.) Find the balance by mixing it up.

Fail #4: You Just Went Heavy on Him

Oh snap! If you went heavy, it's going to take some serious work on your part to come back from it. In fact, this might be one of the hardest fails to fix once the deed's been done. Worse, there are so many ways that it can occur!

Generally, going heavy means throwing an excessive amount of heaving, perspiring, ugly emotion or demands on top of him like a basket of filthy laundry. We've already gone over this in part, but just to reiterate, play smart and avoid comments like:

- I'm disappointed in you.

- Where is this relationship going?

- I'm pretty sick of you at the moment.

- Are you playing games with me?

- I love you
  (if you just told him you love him for the first time in a
    text, you worry me!)

- When do I get to meet your parents?

- You're using me aren't you?

Remember: texting is simply not a good medium to talk about very emotional topics. If you really need to tell this guy something, do so over the phone. It's never appropriate to blast him with some enormous emotional weight via text. How could you ever expect him to respond in a way that would make you happy?

Fail #3: You're Texting Like You're in a Chat Room

Your tiny SMS text box will never replace your AIM chat that you had as a kid. Nor should you ever expect it to feel like a Skype chat room where you fire off messages in short succession to one another. Instead, think of texting like a game of correspondence chess. This kind of chess can be played in the mail (old school!) or more commonly online. One person moves a piece, and the next person moves some hours, days, or even weeks afterward. Given, you want to give him a response earlier than a week from when he texts you, but you get my drift.

It's a slow process, but it's important that we drag our feet a bit in this regard. It's a conversation done at great length, with short bursts of content that are used to meet up, flirt, or otherwise increase the good sort of tension. Using it in any other way is going to strain your relationship or bring him to seek an immediate exit.

Save the chat for one-on-one dates. Use texting more as a means of getting together, building tension and respect.

Fail #2: You've Become Too Apologetic

Yes, a person can say "I'm sorry" too much, and this knee-jerk reaction tends to happen way more often in relationships where the balance is tilted toward one person or another. The effects, unfortunately, can be devastating.

Saying sorry in the wrong circumstances is going to make you appear weak-willed and not confident. It is not attractive at all if said over and over again to someone, and eventually it leads that person to realize that you don't have much to offer in way of value.

I teach men and women to eliminate the "I'm sorry" statement unless you REALLY fucked up.

So, be on the lookout for loose apologies, especially in text form! You'd be surprised at how a quick show of charm can dispel the need of saying sorry to someone. For example:

You: So big fella, hitting the gym with me today?

Him: Was thinking of relaxing actually!

You: Just you and a bag of Cheetos, eh? Am I invited later or is this a three's a crowd kind of thing?

Him: Still on my diet...does it look like I hang around all day and do nothing?

> *You: No no...I didn't mean anything by it. I was just kid-*
> *ding, sorry.*

I need one of those error buzzers right about now. She was doing so good until BUZZZZ, she apologized for a bit of very obvious sarcasm and flirting. She even asked if she could come over and see him!

What happened here is that she assumed the worst, something we are all prone to doing, especially when someone we like is in the mix. It is very probable that this guy is actually playing along with the conversation, throwing in a bit of his own sarcasm to add to the conversation. Given, a smiley face would have been a good touch, but in essence you should trust that your comment's wit got through his thick skull. (If you're ever unsure, add a smiley face of your own! That will remove all doubt.)

If you're faced with a situation like this, **go along with it!** Add to the conversation, but instead of apologizing, throw in another sassy comment:

> Him: Still on my diet...docs it look like I hang around
>   all day and do nothing?

> *You: Hardly! You could go toe to toe with Chuck Norris*
>   *and he would only just barely beat you!*

This does a couple of things. If he really did feel defensive about your previous comment, this will dispel it entirely with an injection of humor. And if he was playing with you in the first place, you followed up with a witty comment of your own and scored major points with him.

Lastly, there was one other point that I wanted to make, and that was with the use of JK, or just kidding. It's the same damn thing as sorry. It takes a flirty comment with all of its passion and fun and dilutes it into a boring watery beverage. Stay away from these kinds of comments and be bold! It will take you far.

Fail #1: You Double Texted

Texting twice is about as desperate as you can get. Given, we've all been there, and yes it can be agonizing if you've said something important and you're waiting for a response. But that is all the more reason to keep the important stuff out of texting. If you're keeping things light and fun, you can go about your day without feeling a pit in your stomach worrying about his response.

In very rare instances, it's okay to double text if you want to break up a big text, or add something quickly (as in under a minute). But if you are sending texts and then sending more after not receiving a response, you're going to show yourself to be too impatient and too clingy.

Do yourself a favor and let him respond. Do not under any circumstances try to tell yourself some lie about how your text never made it to him.

You: Hey, you going out tonight?

Him: No response

You: Did you get my text?

Of course he got it! The odds of your digital SMS text message being lost in the ether of electromagnetic static is so miniscule it doesn't exist. Yes, you can tell yourself that he lost his phone. But if he lost it he's going to find some other way of contacting you later. Just wait patiently for the text. In the meantime your job is to keep yourself from thinking the worst, and to just let things play themselves out for the next few days.

If you can successfully NOT do the ten things I just mentioned above, then you're going to be a textpert in no time. Just keep your head about you and follow these guidelines. I promise they will never steer you wrong!

CHAPTER 5:

The First Dates and Beyond –
Romancing by Text

We're bringing it all together in chapter 5! This final chapter dedicated to tying in everything that we've learned up until now. Chapter 5 starts off with important tips and tricks regarding those first few dates. I'll follow this up with a segment on how to keep a great texting game going long after you and your man have moved into a new stage of the relationship.

First Contact:
When Should I Go For It and Should I Text or Call?

Ah, the age old question of when to knock out that first text or call! Too soon and you risk sending an implicit message that you are needy. Send it too late and he will not be sure who you are.

More and more often people are choosing texting over calling as their initial contact method. The reasons behind this are simple: it looks less needy for one, and two, it can be far, far less awkward. Calling someone new is terrifying. Sending them a text is not.

When to send out that first text is another issue entirely. If you ask, you're going to get a million different opinions. The more prudent among us use the mainstay three day rule. You wait three days before you text or call. But if you talk to someone younger, you're likely to get an entirely different response. In fact you might get laughed at if you bring it up.

The younger crowd is more intent on getting the ball rolling quickly. If they want to get to know someone they are going to make it happen. My belief is that they are as intent as everyone else to make it work, but they are less interested in following "three day rules" or "three date rules or whatever other rules people have come up with. And being a young guy myself (at heart that is!) I feel I have to concur with them.

You may choose to side with caution, in which case I'd say stick to three days. If you're feeling bold, rebellious and out of control with the violence and passion of youth, go with two! And while I know some people will text the next day, to me, the infinitely wise dating coach, it reeks of **impatience** and **need** and I'd stay away from such tactics unless you're just out to get some, in which case I'd say go for it!

I'll conclude this segment with a point of clarification: **of course you can text him first.** Given, if you do, you want to make absolutely sure you play it cool as a cucumber from there on out. Another reason to wait three days is because he is much more likely to text you first if you wait that long, sparing you the worry of having to text first. But nowadays, it's quite common for the girl to go first, and it doesn't diminish your guy from feeling alpha, as long as you let him take the lead afterward.

- So wait 2-3 days and see if he texts you.

- Then, if he doesn't, feel free to text him some wit.

- If you can't wait, then text him using one of my seductive techniques at the beginning of the book.

How to textpress yourself in that first message

He may text you first or you may text him. If you go first, one of the best options is to tie in that text with how you met. Maybe you met at a party, so you have a mutual friend. Maybe you met at a rock concert, or a bar downtown. If that first response can establish a connection right off the bat, congrats—that's a first rate job!

You: Hey it's Kerry. Rockin' party! How's the hangover? :-)

Or...

You: Hey there it's Laura. Had a blast the other night... still at Betty Ford, didn't even know that bar existed before my friends dragged me there!

Use humor and let things flow like you've known him forever. This immediately breaks the ice between you and can really get those sparks flying right off the bat!

You: Gotta say it...out of all the guys (and girls ha!) I gave my number to the other night you were my fav :-)

This is bold, humorous, flattering, and fun. It puts the ball in his court to respond in the same manner, letting you both relax a little! And as a bonus he is turned on by the fact he thinks you're bi!

Another consideration is to think about what you want from the relationship before you send off that first text. If you're looking for a hookup, games aren't worthwhile or necessary. Setting up a quick date at a bar after 10 PM is a pretty obvious sign of where things are going. However, if you want something more, then you'll want to remember that each text should be building either tension in your relationship or respect through boundaries.

And as a final tip: if you need some practice, practice on guys you aren't all that interested in! Practice texting a guy and see how he reacts—you may find the right combination to use in the future by making this Guinea Pig your test model.

Setting Up Dates

I've already gone over setting up dates in previous chapters. However I wanted to sum up everything here and give you a few more ideas.

First, don't be afraid to ask for a different time. I tell my guys to boldly hit you with a day and hour. Specifics are very important! If you like him, avoid general comments like "sometime soon" or "we'll get something set up." These comments are there for women who **don't want to go out with a guy.**

However, if you can't make it, or you want to set up some early sign of your independence and value, then say you've got plans **but** hit him with another possible time and date. Remember: he instigated the idea of a date. You don't need to play coy here—there are better times to do so.

If the date is a few days away, it doesn't hurt to send one text between when you first set up the date and when you actually go on it. Usually this can be in the form of a confirmation:

You: Excited for tomorrow. You wouldn't know if they have good martinis would you? :-)

Him: They happen to have the best Bombay Sapphire martini in the city. So I'd say you're in luck!

You: Not good...now I'll need more than one!

This is a great way to confirm a date by saying you're excited for it, and then asking him a question about it. If you had just said "hey, we still on for tomorrow?" it sounds a bit unfriendly, almost as if you're accusing him of standing you up before you even get there. Not good!

Finally, if you don't receive a response from your first text, or the guy hasn't texted you after that week mark, I'd suggest backing off and letting that one go. Similarly, gauge the tone of his texts. They might be extremely brief, or perhaps he hasn't even mentioned going on a date with you. Maybe he's texting you at 1 AM asking to see you. These are all obvious signs that he's not going to work out. Either he's simply uninterested or he's already got a girlfriend.

Don't worry if this happens! Hooking a fish and getting it into your boat are two entirely different things. Not even the experts can catch them all.

Texting After the First Date

If you had dinner with him, I'd avoid texting him the very same night! However, the morning after doesn't hurt. Make sure you use specifics. I don't want to see you typing things like:

- Had a great time John

- Was a lot of fun. We have to do it again sometime!

- Thanks for dinner :-)

Vague and uninteresting, all of these. Focus on the specifics, and if you can point out something fun that happened that night that made it worthwhile.

- Awesome time Mr. Rick that band rocked!

- Seeing you down that fruity girls drink was a real turn on last night. :-)

- Snap! That was FUN. Would have been perfect if the Bruins hadn't been idiots and thrown the game!

The last quote is definitely the shit! If you went out to a sports bar and watched a game with him (and were genuinely interested), he is probably already buying a ring.

You get the drift. Stick with comments that show real interest in how things went that night. Specifics are a good way to show you cared. Leave the general stuff to the losers that didn't work out.

Pro Texting Tips!

Just because you've broken all that ice doesn't mean you'll get smooth sailing! Far from it, the next few dates will definitely keep you on your toes as the two of you get to know each other. And of course, one of the ways people can show their character is through how they text.

Maybe they text too much. If so, they're likely clingy. Maybe they text too little. Perhaps they're uninterested. Maybe they send you boring texts after you send funny ones. They're probably boring! You can learn a ton, and because he's probably never read a book on texting and you have, you already have the upper hand on him.

And that's never a bad thing!

Let's check out a few master-level tips that I've come across over my years of using texting. Keep these in mind and I guarantee they will never steer you wrong!

Pro Tip #1: The Automatic Responder

Wouldn't it be great if you could get him to respond right away to something you said? You could potentially use this to reignite a relationship that is flailing in the early stages, or perhaps you need a side conversation to initiate a conversation about a date.

At times like these, you want a way to get him responding immediately!

There's a few ways you can do this. First, you can provide him with something that he really wants to know about. We've talked about this earlier, where you use a brief snippet of information to really capture his interest:

- Ran into someone who said he knew you from high school!

- Do you know anyone working at MidTown Bar?

- Had a dream about you the other night!

- You've got some...intriguing pictures of you up on Facebook :-)

In all of these, you've piqued his interest. You've engaged him. His ego DEMANDS an answer! You can expect he is wondering who the hell you met or what in the world you saw that made you mention something. When he writes back, play it cool and never quite tell him what or who you saw.

Another possibility is to hook him with information that you know he would enjoy. Say he likes surfing for example:

> *You: Hey check this out. Awesome article I found on surfing! Did you know there was a tournament held there ever year?*

> Him: Had no idea! But now I want to go!

> *You: Well you could definitely fly to Hawaii. Or you could watch it at Encore Sports Bar with me next week :-)*

This tends to work because you're focusing on the things that interest him. You've shown that you take him seriously and you want to know more about why he likes what he likes. Guys **love** explaining things to girls. Ask questions and you'll get a response.

Lastly, force him to respond with some serious teasing. Let's say you see something that reminds you of him, but you want to tease him about it. For example:

> *You: I saw a dog pissing on a tree just now and it reminded me of you having to pee 40 times last night.*

Unless he is really, really uninterested in you, he is **going** to respond to that. If his interest was flagging, this slight bit of tension may jog his senses and make him come to his senses and see what an awesome girl you are.

Pro Tip #2: Making the Most of Emoticons

At this point you've all seen plenty of smiley faces and sad faces in the examples of this texting book. They are incredibly useful tools, and are capable tone softeners that no great texter can do without.

Besides emoticons, there are also certain acronyms like lol or rofl that you can use which ensure that your sarcastic comment doesn't come off the wrong way. It's difficult to gauge how someone will see your text, so when in doubt, use a tone softener!

There's nothing worse than sending a super sarcastic text over and then having the guy not respond. You're left wondering whether he really thought you were serious, which in turn makes it extremely difficult to resist a second text to apologize. And as you certainly know by now, double texting and apologizing are more often than not **bad** things that you must avoid doing.

A last word with emoticons: they can be overused. If you start sending smiley faces over with every single text, then they are going to be ignored when you really need one. Think of your smiley faces as strategic tools used only when you desperately need one to clarify your intent. In all other cases your content itself will be enough.

Pro Tip #3: Hit Him with a Nickname

Nicknames a great! First, they can be used to tease your man remorselessly. In most cases they are slightly insulting, which puts you in a power position and gives you cred in the relationship. Even the simple use of Mr. before their first name is both amusing and teasing. Eventually, a nickname can become a term of endearment that mean a lot to both parties.

Feel free to recycle good nicknames for guys you meet. I enjoy using lamb chop—it hasn't failed me yet!

Of course, finding them can be difficult at first, but the more dates you go on with the guy, the more chances you have of inventing one. Unfortunately nicknames are like Eureka moments. They pop into your head as if by magic. What I'm saying is there's no use waiting around for it. Get to know him and you'll eventually find a great one.

Pro Tip #4: Hitting the Pause Button before Sending

If you've ever sent a text and then immediately regretted it, you know how incredibly useful a pause button would have been about then. But because you know there isn't one, it pays to stop before you press send, go over everything one last time, and then, for good measure, leave it in draft form and let it sit there for a while!

We get emotional. We want to tell people things. And while that's perfectly fine and good, there's a time and a place for it. Be very cautious about sending something if you're emotional. If you have any doubts, put it away for a while and let it sit. You may open it back up later and be appalled by what you were going to send.

As a side benefit, reading your text at least once more will help you identify spelling errors and such that to any educated guy will be obvious and potentially harmful (although he would have to be a real Grammar Nazi to pick on you for some tiny error!)

Text Etiquette

Ladies, if you're in your 20's you're probably texting freaks. I teach my guys to not get offended when you're on a date with them and you're texting up a storm. I tell them to not tell you to stop, and definitely not to ask who you're texting. Fair is fair: you should pay a similar favor to the guys you're with, or else you'll be looking like a nut job.

I understand why you do it and I have more than a few ways of keeping you in check, but you have to admit...the guys that write me aren't too keen on getting ignored. In the end I just tell them to step up their game or ignore you back.

No one likes being ignored. Even if you aren't trying to hurt his feelings, you have to admit that this looks bad. When you're on a date, try to keep the phone use to a minimum. You never know—the guy you're with could write you off forever for pulling a stunt like that.

Common Backfire Moments: "Can I Come Back from This?"

Now, I'm not often a betting man, but if I were I'd say that you're going to get yourself in trouble every now and then with a bad text. Either you sent something to him that you immediately regretted, or you showed yourself to be (ever so slightly) unhinged, or perhaps you simply expressed too much interest, or too little.

It happens to the best of us. Dating, like everything else, is a skill that we get better at with time. Of course, when you're dealing with love, it can be much harder to walk away from a mistake. But when you take it too far, **taking a step back is the only way to have a chance at repairing the mistake.** If you run and apologize to him you will almost **never** succeed!

I'm going to go over a few common problems that you may run across when you're texting your man. But to put it bluntly: if you've done anything on this list, it's in your best interest to halt all contact and move on. That advice probably hurts, but at least it's going to put your head in the right place and get the healing process started.

You waited too long to respond and he seems uninterested...
A girl I spoke with recently had mentioned this. She had been playing smart by keeping her texts spaced out with lots of time between his responses and hers, but she thought she had gone too far and left him hanging too long, eventually leading her man stopped texting her altogether. So she overcorrected **again** by texting twice without a response.

It's a tough break. To ensure that it doesn't happen, play by the rule that you wait exactly how long he waited to text you back, plus an hour. This way you stay around his interest level, and show just a little less for good measure.

As for this gal here, if she texted twice without a response, it's likely over. You simply cannot send another text without losing face even more and looking like a weirdo. You **might** be able to salvage the situation if you wait a week and then respond with something. This can work as a "reset" of sorts, but it really is hit or miss and more often than not it's a miss.

You said the "L" word or something like it...

Actually either "like" or "love" fits into the "L" word category. You **must** not express this unless you are absolutely sure he reciprocates it. Or better yet, he says it first.

You have to **coax** a guy into these things. If you say you love him first, you rocked the boat and you can't recover without some serious rebalancing. How do you rebalance? Well, if he stopped responding to you shortly after you mentioned it, chances are you're done. If you know where he hangs out you can pull the jealousy card and talk to other guys when he's around. This can tip the balance more toward you, but it doesn't necessarily correct things.

You **must** play it cool from here on out. Correcting that mistake can take a month or more. It's like a wolf sticking it's foot into the same trap twice. After some time has gone by and the trap has been relocated, you may still have a chance to snag your alpha wolf.

You tried to guilt trip him into a response...

He isn't showing you the same feelings you have for him, so you try to pressure him into feeling them. Of course you know that this **cannot** work **ever**! Even if it does he will resent you for it and be looking for a way out.

Let's say you throw out some casual "I don't care but I really do care" response like "That's fine, don't respond to my message. Have better things to do anyway." He isn't fooled by this. It's a terrible attempt to get him to need you, and because need is more often than not a very ugly thing to behold, you get blacklisted, this time for good.

Recovery is likely impossible. Yes, you can try waiting a week or so, but this comment was rude and final. Texting him back after this with a light comment would sound absurd. If you are in a situation like this, do yourself a favor: learn from the mistake and move on. It's the absolute best that can happen here.

Power Texting – Final Thoughts

Texting is an incredible dating platform, and when used properly it can do everything from spicing up a relationship to promoting respect and value. As a dating coach I put a huge focus on becoming good at it, because it's not going out of style any time soon. In fact, it's only getting more popular.

In the beginning texting is **crucial**. Enter your text and then look at it (before sending) and ask yourself this question:

- Could this text come from any other girl? If yes, your text SUCKS. Make him remember you with some wit! Take a chance and don't play it so safe. You have other men right? You want one that will come out and play on your terms and in your playground! If he can't handle a neg or laugh at your joke while texting then he is a boring loser.

Keep it short, keep it pithy and above all make it unique!

I hope you enjoyed the eBook as much as I enjoyed writing it. As a final piece of advice, never forget that **you are in control of the text.** You run the game, and you do it by matching his interest at first, and then decreasing that interest ever so slightly, so that **he** is always the one chasing **you**. If you take any other approach, it won't be long before the balance is skewed and you'll be out of business (at least until you find another great looking stud!).

AUTHOR'S
BIO

So as I'm sure you ladies know by now, my name is Gregg. And what you've probably guessed at over the course of this book is that I've had a lot of time to be single and, yes, to enjoy it! Now, that doesn't mean that I haven't taken a walk down relationship road once or twice. It's just that for me, being single is the state of mind that I find most agreeable. And who wouldn't? If you've finished reading my book, you'll realize that being single is a great way to experience new things and meet amazing new people. What's not to like about that!

If you ever get a chance to meet me, you'll quickly find that I'm a pretty friendly and generous (maybe too generous!) guy. In fact, I'm often showing that very same generosity by letting my friends stay at my place when their relationships take turns for the worst. While a buddy of mine is recovering, we tend to have a little fun, you know, to take his mind off things. We pal around for a few months, but soon enough my friends find other cuties that are worth settling down for.

This scenario happens quite a bit, enough times at least for my buddy Keith to tell me "Gregg, you've helped out so many of us at one point or another. Why don't you start a dating site?" Two years ago, I took him up on that advice, and my website KeysToSeductions.com was born. Its success has been amazing, and today I have over a hundred pages of content and 1000 unique visitors every day.

Why is the site so successful? I think it has something to do with me being a true natural when it comes to meeting and talking to women. I'm not sure how I hit on that particular skill. It may have been luck. Or you could chalk it up to the fact that I had three older sisters that tortured me when I was a little runt. I didn't have much interest in reading dating books, and when I finally got around to them I found that they were taught poorly and offered little to no engagement. I knew I could do better.

The goal of KeysToSeductions, by the way, was to help men build their confidence enough to really get out there and start finding women of value. In a way, the advice I give to both men and women has more similarities than differences. Confidence and self-worth are critical, and stands behind everything I teach.

For the average guy that I write to at least, this is exactly what they need: confidence. Hell, I'm an average guy! I'm average height and average looking—and yet I love going up against Mr. Tall, Dark and Handsome and winning! I taught myself how to dance and that, along with making women laugh, is my social edge.

As for why I'm writing to women...the truth is that it was a natural next step. Being completely sincere here: I love and respect women, I honestly do. I have no interest in manipulating them, nor would I ever need to. Over the years, I've listened to what women have to say. I know them inside and out. I've been doing the dating coach thing and the single thing for so long now that it's safe to say I understand what gets under your skin, and what the biggest problems are with your dating lives.

No, I haven't dated the hottest supermodels alive and no, I haven't been from one TV show to the next promoting myself and my skillset in this regard. For the most part I'm quite private, and I like it like that. Still, my coaching takes me everywhere, from California to Nevada to Florida. It's a life I love to lead; and even though I often end up missing home (I grew up in Boston, and today I have homes in West Palm and Las Vegas) it's still the only life I can imagine leading.

MORE BOOKS

By Gregg Michaelsen

For Women

**The Social Tigress:
Dating Advice for Women
to Attract Men and Get a Boyfriend**

**Who Holds the Cards Now?
5 Lethal Steps to Win His Heart and Get Him to Commit**

**How to Get Your Ex Back Fast!
Toy with the Male Psyche and Get Him Back
with Skills only a Dating Coach Knows**

For Men

**From Zero to Hero:
A Modern Guy's Guide to
Understanding a Woman's Heart
(with Kat Kingston)**

**Hook, Line & Date Her:
The Average Guy's Book
to Attract, Meet and Date Quality Women**

**The Building of a Confident Man:
How to Create Self Esteem
and Become More Attractive to Women**

Find them on Amazon today!

Printed in Great Britain
by Amazon